WORLD  CULTURES

Yanomami

CHRISTINE WEBSTER

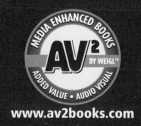

MEDIA ENHANCED BOOKS

AV²
BY WEIGL™

ADDED VALUE • AUDIO VISUAL

www.av2books.com

AV² provides enriched content that supplements and complements this book. Weigl's AV² books strive to create inspired learning and engage young minds in a total learning experience.

Your AV² Media Enhanced books come alive with...

Audio
Listen to sections of the book read aloud.

Key Words
Study vocabulary, and complete a matching word activity.

Video
Watch informative video clips.

Quizzes
Test your knowledge.

Embedded Weblinks
Gain additional information for research.

Slide Show
View images and captions, and prepare a presentation.

Try This!
Complete activities and hands-on experiments.

... and much, much more!

Go to **www.av2books.com**, and enter this book's unique code.

BOOK CODE

T 8 2 5 9 4 7

AV² by Weigl brings you media enhanced books that support active learning.

Published by AV² by Weigl
350 5th Avenue, 59th Floor
New York, NY 10118

Website: www.av2books.com   www.weigl.com

Library of Congress Cataloging-in-Publication Data
Webster, Christine.
  Yanomami / Christine Webster.
    p. cm. — (World cultures)
  Includes index.
  ISBN 978-1-62127-508-4 (hardcover : alk. paper) — ISBN 978-1-62127-512-1 (softcover : alk. paper)
  1. Yanomamo Indians—Juvenile literature. I. Title.
  F2520.1.Y3W42 2013
  305.898'92—dc23
                              2012041038

Printed in the United States of America in North Mankato, Minnesota
1 2 3 4 5 6 7 8 9 0 17 16 15 14 13

052013
WEP170513

Senior Editor Aaron Carr
Art Director Terry Paulhus

Photo Credits
Every reasonable effort has been made to trace ownership and to obtain permission to reprint copyright material. The publishers would be pleased to have any errors or omissions brought to their attention so that they may be corrected in subsequent printings.

Weigl acknowledges Getty Images, Dreamstime, and iStockphoto as primary photo suppliers for this title.

CONTENTS

Where in the World?

GUYANA

VENEZUELA

BRAZIL

ATLANTIC OCEAN

PACIFIC OCEAN

SOUTH AMERICA

ATLANTIC OCEAN

LEGEND

Yanomami distribution

N
W E
S

SCALE

0   125 Miles

0   125 Kilometers

Continent: South America
Population: 385,742,554
Indigenous Population (Yanomami): About 32,000
Nations: Brazil and Venezuela
Area of South America: 6,878,000 square miles (17,814,000 square kilometers)

The Yanomami are a group of **indigenous peoples** from South America. The word *Yanomami* means "human being." Yanomami are sometimes referred to as Yanomama, Yanomano, or Yanoama. These Native Peoples, who live deep in the **Amazon** rainforest, were not discovered by other cultures until the 1950s. Although most people in the world use modern technology, there are a few **cultures** that continue to live as they did hundreds of years ago. The Yanomami are one such group. They had very little contact with other cultures until the 1980s. By living deep in the dense jungle of the Amazon rainforest, the Yanomami have been able to **preserve** a culture that is more than 8,000 years old. The Yanomami are the largest indigenous group living in the Amazon Basin who still practice their ancient traditions.

The Amazon Basin is home to thousands of different kinds of animals and plants. There can be hundreds of different types of trees in just 1 square mile (2.6 sq. km) of the Amazon rainforest.

About 25,000 Yanomami live in the mountainous areas bordering southern Venezuela and northern Brazil. Scattered among enormous trees, there are about 225 Yanomami villages. Their territory extends from the Orinoco River in Venezuela to the Northern Perimetral highway in Brazil. Since the Yanomami live apart from **societies** that use modern technology, they have their own technology which uses only the natural resources found in the Amazon Basin. They have survived for thousands of years by farming, hunting, and fishing the area around the Amazon River.

Culture Cues

🐆 The Amazon rainforest is the largest rainforest in the world. Two-thirds of the Amazon rainforest is located in Brazil.

🐆 The average temperature in the Amazon rainforest is 80° Fahrenheit (27° Celsius).

🐆 The Amazon rainforest is home to about 250,000 kinds of plant life.

🐆 The Amazon River is almost 4,160 miles (6,695 kilometers) long. Its water **volume** is 11 times that of the water volume of the Mississippi River.

Stories and Legends

Yanomami legends are told to explain where the animals and plants of the Amazon come from. The Yanomami also tell stories to entertain each other.

Many cultures believe that there is a separation between the physical and **spiritual** worlds. The Yanomami do not make this separation. They believe there is no barrier between the physical world and the spiritual world.

The Yanomami believe that the world has four layers. The top layer is called the *duku ka misi*. Many things are created on this layer. The second layer is called the *hedu ka misi*, or the "sky layer." The Yanomami believe that this layer is similar to Earth, with animals, plant life, and villages. They also believe that after they die, their **souls** travel to the second layer. The third layer is called the *hei ka misi*, or "this layer." This is where the Yanomami peoples, along with animals and plants, live. Hei ka misi was created when a piece of the hedu ka misi layer broke off. The fourth layer is called *hei ta bebi*. No plants or animals live on the hei ta bebi layer. Instead, the Yanomami believe that **cannibals** live on this layer. These cannibals capture and eat the souls of children.

The Yanomami believe that people and animals share the same souls. For example, a jaguar and a man might have the same soul. Yanomami hunters will not kill a jaguar out of fear that they would be killing one of their own people.

Jaguars appear in many of the Yanomami's stories and legends.

Often, Yanomami myths teach a lesson or explain why something exists. One Yanomami myth explains how human beings were created and why there are so few Yanomami peoples compared to people of European **ancestry**. According to myth, the Moon ate the souls of little children. Villagers became angry at the Moon. A Yanomami named Suhirina shot the Moon with a bamboo-tipped arrow. This caused the Moon to spill blood. The Moon's blood covered Earth. Human beings were formed from this blood. The Yanomami believe the Europeans were created from the thick blood at the center of Earth. This explains why there are so many people of European ancestry. The Yanomami were created from droplets of blood, which explains why their villages have so few people. According to this myth, it is the Moon's blood that causes people to fight and kill one another.

THE STORY OF
How the Yanomami Got Plantains

At one time, the Yanomami did not know that they could eat plantains. Only a man named Boreawa knew how to grow and harvest plantains. He did not teach others how to use the plantains. Instead, they ate other plants. Boreawa hid the plantains in the forest.

Soon, other people learned about the plantains. During a heavy rainfall, Horonama got lost in the forest. As he searched to find the way back to his village, he found Boreawa's hidden plantains.

Horonama did not know what to do with the plantains. After some time, he discovered that he could eat them. He thought they were a very tasty fruit. Horonama asked Boreawa how to grow the fruit. Boreawa taught Horonama how to grow the plantains. The Yanomami still grow plantains. They are an important part of the Yanomami diet.

About 30,000 years ago, the Yanomami's ancestors traveled to the Amazon Basin from Asia. These peoples adapted to their new environment. They hunted animals and gathered plants in the thick jungles, fished in the Amazon River, and planted small gardens. After the arrival of Christopher Columbus in 1498, many other indigenous groups died from the illnesses brought by Europeans visiting the Amazon Basin. The Yanomami were unharmed by these diseases because the Europeans did not travel deep enough into the forest to reach them. Nearly 300 years later, in 1760, Spanish soldiers reached the edges of the Yanomami's land. The Yanomami were known to be fierce fighters. The soldiers were afraid to fight these indigenous peoples, so they did not travel through the Yanomami's land. Explorers did not return to the area for another 150 years.

Timeline of the Yanomami

30,000 Years Ago Yanomami ancestors travel to South America via the Bering Strait.

1950s Anthropologist Napoleon Chagnon travels among the Yanomami peoples, learning about their culture.

1726 Europeans arrive on Yanomami land.

1498 Christopher Columbus lands in the Americas; About 2 million indigenous peoples are located in the Amazon Basin.

1760s Spanish explorers reach the outskirts of Yanomami land.

Gold was discovered in the Yanomami region in 1970. This discovery brought many problems to these indigenous peoples. By 1987, about 40,000 miners had flocked to the area in search of this rich mineral. The miners brought diseases, such as **hepatitis, malaria,** and **tuberculosis,** to the area. The Yanomami were not **immune** to these diseases, and many died. The miners destroyed the Yanomami's land, **polluted** their rivers, and even killed some of their people. Since the arrival of the miners, more than 20 percent of the Yanomami population has died.

The Yanomami are one of the more recent cultures to come into contact with the outside world. This contact has brought **devastation** to the Yanomami and their ancient culture. These people now face pollution, disease, loss of land, and, most importantly, they are threatened with the loss of thousands of years of traditions and culture.

1998 Fires sweep through Roraima, Brazil.

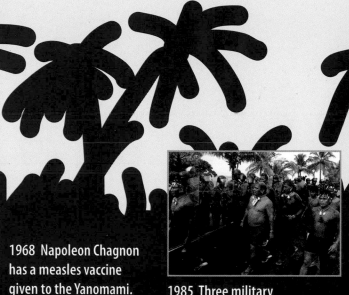

1968 Napoleon Chagnon has a measles vaccine given to the Yanomami.

1985 Three military bases are completed on Yanomami land in Brazil.

1970s Perimetral Norte Road is built, allowing thousands of miners into the Yanomami area.

1992 The Yanomami Indigenous Park is established by the Brazilian government for the Yanomami.

1993 A group of miners attack the Yanomami village Haximu, killing many of the Yanomami.

Social Structures

The Yanomami believe that everything in the world has a spirit and is alive. They believe that if they care for the land and use it wisely, it will provide for them. They also believe that the **fate** of all people is linked to the fate of the environment. This ties to the belief that by destroying the environment, society is killing itself.

In Yanomami society, only men are allowed to become a shaman. All men are allowed to try to become a shaman, but the process is difficult, and not many men succeed.

Each Yanomami community has at least one spiritual leader called a shaman. To become a shaman, a Yanomami man receives intense training. During this time, the trainee fasts, or eats only small amounts of food, for at least 1 year. He loses much weight. An older man teaches the trainee the songs, rituals, and practices of the shaman.

According to Yanomami **mythology,** the sky is ancient and full of many holes. If a shaman did not continue his work in the Yanomami community, the sky would fall apart. The Yanomami also believe that a shaman can contact the spirit world and cure illnesses. A shaman may make mixtures of jungle plants that, when eaten, bring visions of the spirit world. The Yanomami believe a shaman can use the power of the spirits to cure disease. The Yanomami believe that the world will end if these practices disappear.

The curassow is a bird that lives only in the tropical rainforest. It can grow to be more than 3 feet (91 cm) long.

The Yanomami believe that birds often spread culture to human beings. They believe birds taught human beings how to make fire. They also believe that birds taught human beings which plants are safe to eat. The Yanomami believe that birds, like humans, have their own places and habits.

This connects birds and humans spiritually. Birds live in the heavens, and connect Earth and the spirit world. Curassows, macaws, parrots, and toucans are a few types of birds considered sacred by the Yanomami. Their feathers are often used to make ceremonial headgear.

THE TWO SEASONS

The Yanomami of the Amazon identify two seasons instead of four. During the wet season, large amounts of rainfall make it difficult to travel the land. During the dry season, the Yanomami travel to each other's villages for ceremonies and feasts.

Communication

Having lived far from other cultures for so many years, the Yanomami language has remained unchanged. Their language is not like the languages spoken by the indigenous peoples of any other Native groups in the Amazon Basin. Linguists, people who study languages, have learned that present-day Yanomami peoples speak the same language as the first Yanomami groups to settle in the area. This supports the belief that present-day Yanomami are **descended** from the people who traveled from Asia to Amazon Basin about 30,000 years ago.

The Yanomami have one distinct language and four sub-languages within their culture. Traditionally they had no written language, only oral, or spoken, communication. Recent education programs have helped them create a written language. They sometimes use the same word to describe many different things. For example, the Yanomami word *xawara* can mean "disease," "**epidemics**," and "gold."

There are several dialects, or differences, within the Yanomami language. However, each dialect is similar, and people from different villages are able to communicate.

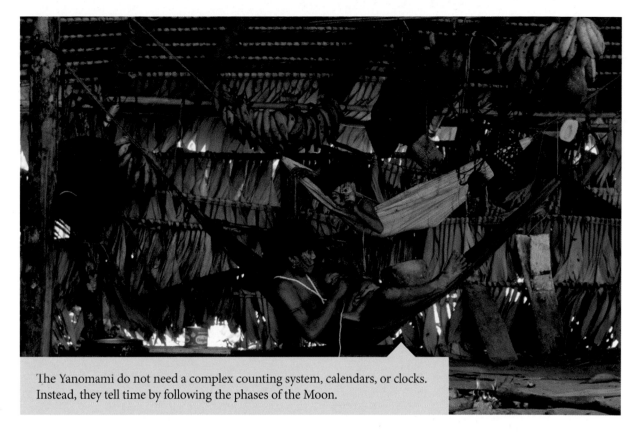

The Yanomami do not need a complex counting system, calendars, or clocks. Instead, they tell time by following the phases of the Moon.

Instead of using a written language, the Yanomami communicate by chanting, dancing, telling stories, and using lively expressions. Their counting system is also unwritten. The system is very simple. The numbers they use to count are: one, two, and "more than two."

A DISTINCT LANGUAGE

The Yanomami have one distinct language. Each community speaks a different version of this language.

Traditionally, the Yanomami had no written language. They communicated orally through speech, song, and expressive movements. The Yanomami's only form of written communication was the drawings they paint on their bodies during ceremonies.

Law and Order

Building the community's house is a job that is shared by every member of the community.

The Yanomami culture does not have **politicians** or a police force to keep law and order. Instead, the Yanomami have village leaders. These leaders do not have power over anyone, but they are able to make suggestions about matters of daily life. For instance, the leaders will express their views about how things should be done. The entire village then makes major decisions together.

A Yanomami village is made up of 30 to 100 people. The entire community lives in a large, circular house called a *shabono* or *yano*. It is about 131 feet (40 m) wide and is made from logs, **thatching**, and mud. The center of the house is open and used as a courtyard for dancing and ceremonies. Each family has a separate area and a fireplace for cooking. They hang **hammocks** around the fire.

Disputes between Yanomami villages can happen at any time. To prevent conflict, it is important for villages to befriend one another.

Yanomami villages create alliances, or friendships, with other villages through feasts, ceremonies, marriages, and the offering of gifts. Yanomami groups are less likely to have disputes with groups with whom they trade and feast.

Yanomami villages are very tight-knit communities. Villagers spend most of their time together in the community house.

Sometimes a village will trade a woman to a nearby community as a peace offering, or in exchange for an item they need. Women often marry members of the group they are traded into, strengthening the bond between the two groups. These offerings reduce disputes between villages and help create **allies**. Allies are needed to help fight during wars between opposing villages. Families who are not warring share land.

Men are responsible for the safety of the group, as well as hunting and planting the gardens. Women's duties include caring for the village children, harvesting the gardens, and cooking. Often, when men are away on hunts, women keep the men in their thoughts throughout the day as a means of helping the hunt.

Young children carry drinking water and firewood to the village. They also spend time learning about their natural surroundings, such as the types of plants and animals living in the area.

Yanomami men are taught how to hunt from an early age. Having this skill is essential for the village to have food and protection.

Celebrating Culture

Marriage is an important part of the Yanomami culture. Through marriage, the Yanomami create friendships with neighboring villages, and produce the many children needed to maintain their culture. Each Yanomami village is one group, or a community. Most villages are a community of **kin**. Members try to marry others from this community. For example, they prefer to marry a cousin, or the son or daughter of a **maternal** uncle. This creates a tight bond between village members. Often, when a baby girl is born, her parents prearrange her marriage by selecting a future husband. In some cases, if the parents are unable to raise their daughter, they choose an older husband for their daughter . She is then raised in the community of her future husband. Most women marry after they reach **puberty**, while many men are 20 years of age or older when they marry.

Children are also an important part of the Yanomami culture. The more children living in a village, the more help is provided with chores. To improve the chances of having many children in a short period of time, men are allowed to marry more than one woman. Having numerous children also gives the family name a better chance of continuing.

Yanomami culture is based around nature and uses many natural materials to make toys and tools.

Ceremonies are another important part of the Yanomami culture. Ceremonies are performed for many reasons and are often used to talk to the spirit world. Ceremonial hunts may be acted out to practice catching a specific animal. Sometimes the Yanomami go on long hunting treks with their families. These treks are similar to family holidays. Often, when the daily work is done, the Yanomami will travel to other villages to share stories and socialize with other groups. Family and relationships are an important part of Yanomami culture.

Yanomami often have soup-eating parties to celebrate special occasions, including when entertaining guests or mourning the death of a loved one.

Art and Culture

The Yanomami are skilled weavers. Some of the baskets they weave are quite detailed.

Using the many natural resources found in the jungle, Yanomami women create the objects needed for everyday life. Baskets are one of the most common and useful items Yanomami women make. In many societies, baskets are found in markets or stores. The Yanomami do not purchase baskets at a store. Instead, they use complex weaving methods to make each basket by hand. **Mamure** fiber is used to weave baskets and hammocks.

The Yanomami need baskets to do their daily chores, such as carrying food and firewood from the garden to the village. One basket that the Yanomami women make is called a burden basket. This basket is used to carry items such as fire sticks, firewood, or fish. The burden basket rests on a woman's back like a backpack. It is carried using a strap that wraps around the forehead, making large loads easier to manage. The Yanomami women are so quick at making burden baskets that they can weave them as they are needed. They sometimes add designs, such as geometric patterns, or use dyes to color the baskets.

Baskets are a form of art and are often decorated by the women who make them.

Pottery was once a very important craft in the Yanomami culture, but this art has almost completely disappeared. One pottery item the Yanomami made was the *hapoka*. The hapoka was a plain, bell-shaped pot made from white clay. Lumpy masses of wet clay were dug by hand from riverbanks and other moist areas. Before the clay was used, it was soaked for a few days. **Impurities** were removed, and the clay was cleaned, kneaded like dough, and molded. Today, rather than make clay pots, many modern Yanomami communities trade their handmade items for aluminum pots.

While Yanomami women use the natural resources around them to make much needed items, they also create things for pleasure. Both men and women express themselves through body painting, feather ornaments, and the unique designs they draw on baskets.

The Yanomami also create songs and dances. Often, the Yanomami perform special songs and dances during a feast to ensure the safety of hunters as they travel in search of food.

Craftsmen are held in high regard in Yanomami society. Tools and utensils are valuable items.

BASKET WEAVING

Yanomami women weave baskets from palm fibers. They decorate these baskets with natural paints. They use burden baskets to carry wood and items they gather in the forest. Flat baskets, or *shotos*, are used in the home as serving baskets and trays. Other serving baskets are shaped like bowls. These baskets are modeled after the Universe. They do not have decorative designs.

Dressing Up

Yanomami children enjoy getting dressed up and painting each other for celebrations.

The Yanomami are not ashamed of their nakedness. Since temperatures are often very hot in the Amazon Basin, Yanomami traditionally wear little clothing. In the past, Yanomami wrapped a thin covering around their hips. Over the years, their clothing has changed. Many men wear a type of apron that covers the lower half of their body. Some even wear shorts. Women wear a short, cotton apron or a wide, cotton belt to cover the lower half of their body.

As with many indigenous cultures, **body adornment** is an important part of the Yanomami culture. Beauty is valued among young indigenous peoples, and they express their beauty through personal adornment. Soft feathers are worn on their bodies for special occasions or ceremonies.

The Yanomami decorate their bodies to show art and physical beauty.

Feathers are also worn on the head, in the earlobes, or on the upper arms. These feathers are used to remind the person wearing them of the bird and the relationship between humans and animals. Feathers also provide spiritual power and protection to the Yanomami.

A shaman often wears colorful feathers from the toucan bird. Headpieces are made from the toucan's feathers. These birds are believed to have strong, magical powers. Body painting is also common. The Yanomami use dyes from forest trees and bushes to paint designs and symbols on their bodies. They paint their bodies with different shades of red and purple for rituals and celebrations. For some festivals, the Yanomami cover their bodies with white clay.

Men usually wear colored bracelets made from bird feathers. They also pierce their earlobes with pieces of **cane**, and pierce their noses and lips with thin bamboo sticks. Yanomami women decorate their ears with flowers, palm shoots, and scented leaves. They also use wooden sticks as body adornment. Women decorate their faces with polished wooden sticks. They push a stick sideways through the center of their nose horizontally. They also insert two sticks into either side of the mouth at the corners. The sticks look like whiskers.

PAINTING WITH PLANTS

The Yanomami used the pods from the *urucu* or *onoto* plants to create paint. The crushed seeds from the pods of these plants produced a red color. The Yanomami used this paint to draw designs on their faces and bodies. To make black paint, the Yanomami chewed or crushed charcoal. When a man fights in a war, he often wears black body paint to symbolize death. A woman wears black paint on her cheeks when she is **mourning**. After one year has passed, she can wear red. The combination of body painting and feathers are worn to display a person's artistic talent.

Food and Fun

The Yanomami hunt, fish, and plant gardens for survival. Men go on hunting trips, using long bows to kill animals. Often, boys are brought along to learn important hunting skills. Most of the food the Yanomami need is grown in gardens. To garden, they use a farming method called "shifting cultivation." This process involves clearing a small area of land for their garden. An area is cleared of trees and bushes, and the land is burned. Many types of seeds are then planted in the garden. Bananas, corn, fruits, sugarcane, and sweet potatoes are just a few of the foods the Yanomami grow. Plantains are the most important food in the Yanomami diet. For feasts, they grow a peach palm fruit called *rasha*. The Yanomami also gather wild fruits and nuts. Plants are also used as food and medicine.

Food is a symbol of prestige, or social status. People who produce and share food are held in high regard. The Yanomami have two **classifications** of food. There are "real" foods and "snacks." Foods that are considered real include large types of game animals, such as alligator, lion, or wild boar. Plantains are also real food. Snack foods include fruits, insects, and small birds. When family members and friends are

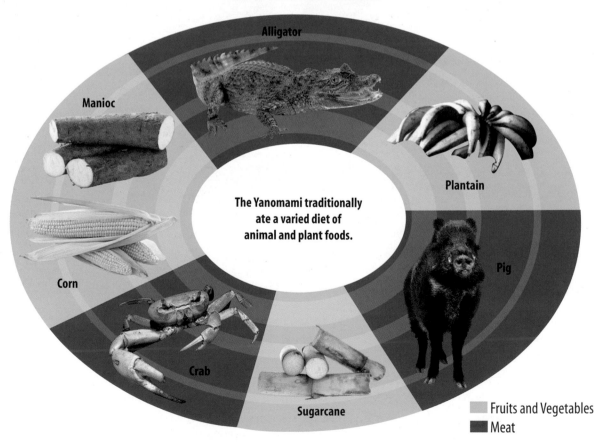

Yanomami Diet

Alligator

Manioc

Plantain

The Yanomami traditionally ate a varied diet of animal and plant foods.

Corn

Pig

Crab

Sugarcane

Fruits and Vegetables
Meat

Manioc is a food that is often eaten by the Yanomami. Manioc is a type of root that is peeled, mashed into a patty, and cooked like a pancake.

invited to a feast, they might be offended if the host does not serve real foods. Mealtimes are more enjoyable when foods are served in large portions.

Ceremonial feasts are important customs in the Yanomami culture. In order to have feasts, communities grow large amounts of food. All of the foods served during a ceremony must come from the host's garden. Although the Yanomami are very careful to have many foods available and enough of them, they are not wasteful. All foods parts are eaten, including the skin and bones of animals. To preserve meat, it is smoked then cooked thoroughly. Meat is boiled for many hours to ensure that it is properly cooked.

While adults gather, hunt, and prepare food, Yanomami children play warrior games. Aside from attending ceremonies, singing, and dancing, games are an important part of a Yanomami child's life. Children play hunting and raiding games. Often, a young boy will use a bow and arrow to shoot small birds or animals. These games are used

to train young warriors so they will be able to provide for their families.

Yanomami men use a bow and arrow to hunt large game. They use spears to catch fish. They must be careful to avoid **piranha** attacks when pulling fish from the water. Women also catch fish. They poison the water with the bark of the *timbo* plant and use their hands to catch fish in holes and burrows.

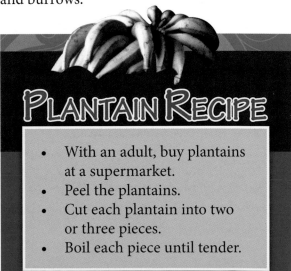

Plantain Recipe

- With an adult, buy plantains at a supermarket.
- Peel the plantains.
- Cut each plantain into two or three pieces.
- Boil each piece until tender.

Great Ideas

The Amazonian poison dart frog is small and colorful, but its poison is extremely dangerous.

Living in the jungle has forced the Yanomami to create tools for hunting. One tool created by the Yanomami is the **blowgun**. A blowgun is made from a piece of cane or tree. A mouthpiece is carved at one end of the cane. Darts are made from sharpened reeds, or tall grass, and placed inside the pole of the gun. A person blows hard into the mouthpiece to shoot the dart at a target. This dart can pierce an animal, but not kill it.

To make the blowgun a more useful hunting tool, the Yanomami came up with an invention involving the poisonous dart frog. They rubbed both sides of a dart in the poison of a poisonous dart frog. When the dart is poisoned, a blowgun is a deadly weapon. A dart shot from a blowgun can travel up to 90 feet (27.4 m) in the air. Its poison is strong enough to kill large game.

Hunting is an important way to obtain food for a culture that does not rely on trade for resources.

Tools and weapons such as the blowgun have helped the Yanomami survive in the jungle for many years.

The bow and arrow is another common tool used by Yanomami men for hunting. They poison arrow tips to make them a more powerful weapon for killing large game.

Most items made by the Yanomami were practical. For example, they used sticks to dig in their gardens.

THE HUNTING BOW AND ARROW

The bow and arrow is one of the most common tools used by the Yanomami to hunt large game. To make a bow, the Yanomami use a **flexible** piece of wood from a palm tree. They use the razor-sharp teeth of a wild pig to shave layers of wood from the bow stave. Bows are very strong and difficult to use. Bow strings are created from handspun fiber that is taken from the inner bark of a tree. A piece of cane is used to make an arrow **shaft**. Feathers are tied to one end of the arrow shaft. An arrowhead is attached to the other end of the shaft. Arrowheads are made from twigs or bones from animals, birds, and fish that have been sharpened to a point.

At Issue

Fishing, hunting, and mining activities have invaded Yanomami land, leaving some Yanomami peoples without the resources they need to survive. Highway and railway development and flooding caused by hydroelectric plants have destroyed other parts of Yanomami land.

At one time, the Yanomami were safe from disease, mining efforts, and technology because they were nestled deep in the forest, far from other cultures. Over time, much has changed, and the Yanomami are now faced with many issues. Among the Yanomami's own villages, their small society faces problems. Sometimes, villages grow quite large. This makes it difficult for the group to remain together through kinship and marriage ties. Many villages break apart. Blood relatives sometimes become enemies. These problems have caused some communities to move away from one another.

Illegal miners have made roads and airplane landing strips on traditional Yanomami lands.

Yanomami culture has been threatened since the gold rush in the late 1980s. Miners have submitted applications to mine 60 percent of Yanomami land. Aside from bringing diseases to the region, miners have caused environmental damage to the land. This activity causes harm to animals—the Yanomami's main means of survival. It also forces them to move their villages. If this harmful activity continues, the Yanomami culture might disappear. Weakened by new illnesses and unable to hunt the land, some Yanomami do not have enough food to survive.

In 1992, the Brazilian government set aside a reservation, or a piece of land, for the Yanomami. This land is called the Yanomami Territory, and the government hopes it will help protect the Yanomami culture from disappearing. Three military bases have since been created on the Yanomami Territory. There are plans to build a fourth military base. This will lead to serious problems among the Yanomami population. Their traditions might be lost as they become more influenced by the outside world.

YANOMAMI LEADER SPEAKS OUT

Davi Kopenawa is a traditional Yanomami leader. He is one of very few Yanomami peoples who have lived outside of the Amazon Basin. Kopenawa was one of the first people to recognize the problems facing these indigenous peoples. He has become a spokesperson—speaking out about gold miners who are destroying the Yanomami Territory and bringing disease to the area. Though Kopenawa is upset that miners are bringing illness and destruction to the territory, he tries to understand why they have come. He hopes to find ways the two cultures can live peacefully together. He believes that change is good for the Yanomami peoples. For example, many have learned to read, write, and protect nature. Kopenawa hopes the Yanomami peoples can study and learn more about modern society. However, he is against the destruction of the land. He hopes miners can find a way to work without cutting down trees and causing oil spills. In 1989, he received the United Nations's Global 500 Award for his efforts.

Into the Future

Although the Yanomami Territory was created in 1992, sometimes the Brazilian government has failed to properly protect this area. Miners continue to enter the Yanomami Territory illegally. In 1993, miners entered one village called Haximu. They attempted to kill the entire village of 85 members. The miners said they were tired of the Yanomami asking for gifts to enter their land. Sixteen Yanomami were killed. Some were women and children. Only two of the miners involved in the killings were jailed.

State and local politicians are trying to reduce the size of the Yanomami Territory. They want access to the rich mineral deposits that are on the land. If this is allowed, single mining workers will be replaced by large-scale, commercial mining operations. The result will be devastating to the Yanomami culture. Logging, cattle ranching, and commercial agriculture are also becoming more common in the area. Clearing land for cattle ranching has caused many forest fires, destroying some of the Yanomami land.

The Yanomami culture was once a well-balanced social system based on trading goods and foods among and between others in their community. Today, the Yanomami must choose between their culture and survival. Since they are new to technology, modern life, and disease, the Yanomami's future is grim. Without protection, they will soon be forced to move from the Amazon Basin to become members of the modern world. Traditions, culture, and a way of life that has been around for thousands of years may soon come to an end.

Much of the Yanomami's territory is in Brazil, which is a modern country with a large population.

Role-play Debate

When people debate a topic, two sides take a different viewpoint about one idea. Each side presents logical arguments to support its views. In a role-play debate, participants act out the roles of the key people or groups involved with the different viewpoints. Role-playing can build communication skills and help people understand how others may think and feel. Usually, each person or team is given a set amount of time to present its case. The participants take turns stating their arguments until the time set aside for the debate is up.

THE ISSUE

For most of their history, the Yanomami lived largely free of contact with the rest of the world. All of that changed in the 1970s when foreign people began flooding into Yanomami lands. The Brazilian government started to build a highway through areas inhabited by the Yanomami. Around this same time, miners from Brazil and Venezuela flocked to the region to mine for tin, gold, and other valuable metals. These people brought with them many diseases, which wiped out large portions of the Yanomami population.

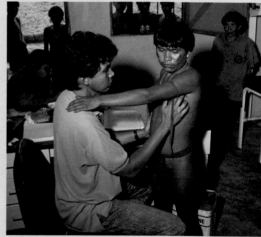

THE QUESTION

Should the governments of Brazil and Venezuela create laws to protect the Yanomami by limit activity in Yanomami lands?

THE SIDES

NO — **Government:** Mining operations provide employment and bring a great deal of money to the economy. The Yanomami can be given protected areas of land to maintain their people and way of life.

YES — **Yanomami:** Mining and other development projects destroy our lands and our traditional way of life, and it will bring diseases that cause the deaths of thousands of our people.

Ready, Set, Go

Form two teams to debate the issue, and decide whether your team will play the role of the government or the role of the Yanomami. Each team should use this book and other research to develop solid arguments for its side and to understand how the issue affects each group. At the end of the role-play debate, discuss how you feel after hearing both points of view.

World Cultures Quiz!

1 What does the word Yanomami mean?

2 In which two South American countries do Yanomami live?

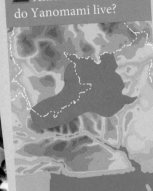

3 What is the estimated current Yanomami population?

4 How long have the Yanomami lived in South America?

5 What discovery brought many foreign people into Yanomami lands in the 1970s?

6 What is a shaman?

7 How do the Yanomami communicate?

8 What is the name of the large, circular homes of the Yanomami people?

9 What is a burden basket?

10 What tool did the Yanomami invent to hunt for food?

ANSWER KEY

1. "human being" **2.** Brazil and Venezuela **3.** 32,000 **4.** About 30,000 years **5.** The discovery of gold **6.** A Yanomami spiritual leader **7.** The Yanomami communication orally, using speech, songs, or expressive movements. **8.** A shabono or yano **9.** A basket Yanomami women use to carry sticks, firewood, or fish **10.** The blowgun

Key Words

allies groups of people who work or fight together

Amazon a river and rainforest in South America

ancestry people, plants, animals, and objects from past generations

blowgun a tube-like weapon that is used to shoot darts

body adornment the practice of decorating the body with symbols and designs that express beliefs and create identity

cane the hard stem of a bamboo plant or other grass plants

cannibals people who eat human flesh

classifications sorted by type

cultures groups of people who share the same customs, values, traditions, and beliefs

descended related to animals, plants, or people from the past

devastation to destroy or cause extreme damage to something

disputes arguments

epidemics diseases or sicknesses that spread quickly

fate a power that causes and controls all events

flexible able to bend without breaking

hammocks beds made from cloth or net that are tied between two poles or trees

hepatitis a liver disease

immune a body that is protected from a disease

impurities to have something mixed into a substance, polluting it

indigenous peoples the first settlers in a particular region or country

kin relatives or family members

malaria a disease caused by a mosquito bite, which causes periods of fever and makes people cold

mamure a plant fiber

maternal the mother's side of the family

mourning feeling sadness because someone dies

mythology ancient stories that explain cultural traditions

piranha a meat-eating fish that has sharp teeth

politicians members of government or organizations that create laws

polluted made something dirty, such as air, land, or water

preserve to keep something safe or to protect something

puberty the stage in life when a child becomes an adult

shaft a long, straight pole that is used as a handle

societies people who live in specific areas and share the same customs and values

souls the spiritual parts of people

spiritual made of or having to do with the spirit; not of the physical world

thatching a roof covering that is made from straw and reeds

tuberculosis a serious disease that attacks a person's lungs

volume the amount of space inside an object

Index

Log on to www.av2books.com

AV² by Weigl brings you media enhanced books that support active learning. Go to www.av2books.com, and enter the special code found on page 2 of this book. You will gain access to enriched and enhanced content that supplements and complements this book. Content includes video, audio, weblinks, quizzes, a slide show, and activities.

AV² Online Navigation

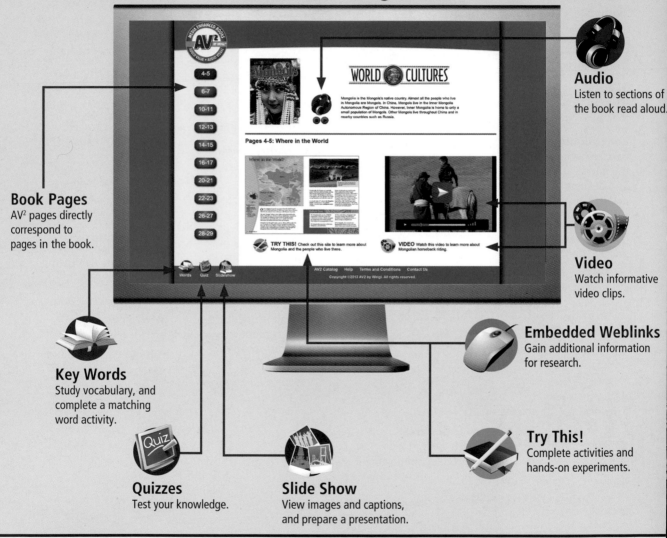

Book Pages
AV² pages directly correspond to pages in the book.

Audio
Listen to sections of the book read aloud.

Video
Watch informative video clips.

Embedded Weblinks
Gain additional information for research.

Key Words
Study vocabulary, and complete a matching word activity.

Try This!
Complete activities and hands-on experiments.

Quizzes
Test your knowledge.

Slide Show
View images and captions, and prepare a presentation.

AV² was built to bridge the gap between print and digital. We encourage you to tell us what you like and what you want to see in the future.

Sign up to be an AV² Ambassador at www.av2books.com/ambassador.